Fact Finders®

AMERICAN INDIAN LIFE

WITHDRAWN

The Ojibwe
The Past and Present of the Anishinaabe

by Alesha Halvorson

Consultant:
Brett Barker, PhD
Associate Professor of History
University of Wisconsin–Marathon County

CAPSTONE PRESS
a capstone imprint

Fact Finders Books are published by Capstone Press,
1710 Roe Crest Drive, North Mankato, Minnesota 56003
www.mycapstone.com

Library of Congress Cataloging-in-Publication Data
Names: Halvorson, Alesha, 1988- author.
Title: The Ojibwe : the past and present of the Anishinaabe / by Alesha
   Halvorson.
Description: North Mankato, Minnesota : Capstone Press, 2016. | Series:
   Fact finders. American indian life | Includes bibliographical references
   and index. | Description based on print version record and CIP data
   provided by publisher; resource not viewed.
Summary: Explains Ojibwe history and highlights Ojibwe life in modern
   society.
Identifiers: LCCN 2015047437 (print) | LCCN 2015043525 (ebook) | ISBN
   978-1-5157-0240-5 (library binding) | ISBN 978-1-5157-0244-3 (pbk.) |
   ISBN 978-1-5157-0248-1 (ebook pdf)
Subjects: LCSH: Ojibwa Indians—History—Juvenile literature. |
   Ojibwans—Social life and customs—Juvenile literature.
Classification: LCC E99.C6 (print) | LCC E99.C6 H28 2016 (ebook) | DDC
   977.004/97333—dc23
LC record available at http://lccn.loc.gov/2015047437

Editorial Credits
Catherine Neitge and Alesha Halvorson, editors; Richard Korab, designer;
Tracy Cummins and Pam Mitsakos, media researchers; Tori Abraham,
production specialist

Photo Credits
Alamy: North Wind Picture Archives, 10, Keith Crowley, 4-5, 26; Capstone
Press: 17; Getty Images: Culture Club, 15 (inset); Granger Historical Picture
Archive: 23, 24; iStockphoto: stacey_newman, 16-17; Library of Congress:
cover (top), 1; Native Stock Pictures: Angel Wynn, cover; Newscom:
Brian Peterson/ZUMAPRESS, 20, Glen Stubbe/ZUMA Press, 18; North
Wind Picture Archives: 13, NativeStock, 27; Shutterstock: AR Images,
19, ekmelica, 22, FotograFFF, 25, fstockfoto, 29, Guoqiang Xue, 6, Helen
Filatova, 4-5 (background), Keith Bell, cover (background), Mark Baldwin,
14; The Image Works: Marilyn Angel Wynn, 8; Wikimedia: Eastman
Johnson/Painting America, 9

Printed in the United States of America.
010653R

Table of Contents

Celebrating Traditions

The sound of a thumping drum fills the air. People of all ages are singing in their native language. A single line of dancers follows in step with the rhythmic heartbeat of the drum. Brightly colored ribbons, beads, and feathers decorate their clothing. After they have gathered in a circle around the drum, a medicine man begins the pipe ceremony. It is a prayer for all of the dancers and for the crowd of visitors. The Grand Entry of the powwow has begun.

Powwows are an important tradition in many American Indian tribes. Ojibwe powwows celebrate life, pride, and the history of a strong group of people. Dancing and singing at powwows carry a deep spiritual meaning for the Ojibwe, who call themselves the Anishinaabe. The powwow ceremony is a time to gather with family and friends to honor, remember, and share Anishinaabe culture.

tradition: custom, idea, or belief passed down through time

Small hawk bells sewed onto puckered moccasins jingle as dancers walk together during the Grand Entry.

Tribal name

Anishinaabe means "original people" in the Algonquian language. The Ojibwe are also known as the Chippewa. Ojibwe and Chippewa come from the Algonquian word *otchipwa*, which means "to pucker." It refers to the distinctive puckered seam of Ojibwe moccasins. Chippewa is used in U.S. treaties and sometimes used as the official tribe name.

Chapter 1

Early Life

The Ojibwe lived in villages throughout the Upper Midwest, near the Great Lakes.

Most Ojibwe lived in the northern Great Lakes region. Their ancestors had lived far to the east. About 1,000 years ago they started a slow migration to the Great Lakes. The Ojibwe mainly lived in what would become the states of Michigan, Minnesota, North Dakota, and Wisconsin and the future Canadian provinces of Ontario and Manitoba.

The Ojibwe were hunter-gatherers and harvested wild rice. They made sugar from the sap of maple trees. Fishing was also a primary source of food. Ojibwe used birch bark for many things, such as food containers, canoes, and to cover their wigwams.

Each season Ojibwe set up homes close to the available food sources. The Ojibwe separated into small bands throughout the seasons so they would not compete for food. When a band moved, their birch bark wigwam coverings were rolled up and taken with them. Typically Ojibwe would return to the same places each year. Ojibwe often rebuilt their homes on the old frameworks left behind the previous year.

ancestor: family member who lived a long time ago
band: group of related people who live and hunt together

FOLLOW THE SEASONS

In the early months of spring, the Ojibwe built their homes near maple trees. They would build the wigwams with hardwood frames and cover them with fresh birch bark and reeds. The Ojibwe tapped maple trees for the sugary sap. Then they boiled the sap into sugar and syrup, which they used to flavor their food.

Toward the end of spring, the Ojibwe moved their camp closer to a nearby lake or stream. Men fished the waters in birch bark canoes and used hand-made spears or nets. In the summer months, men also hunted game, such as birds, deer, and moose. Women and girls gathered berries and plants used for medicine. Together families planted crops, such as beans, squash, and corn. The Ojibwe often stored some of their food, including dried meat and fish, in containers underground to use during the upcoming colder weather.

The Ojibwe camped near lakes or streams in the spring and summer.

WIGWAM DWELLINGS

Ojibwe wigwams were domed or conical dwellings. They varied in size depending on the number of occupants. Poles formed a circular framework. The frame was enclosed with mats made of bark or reeds. A blanket or *hide* covered the wigwam's entrance.

Depending on its size, a wigwam could house one or more families. In larger wigwams more than one campfire could burn at a time. An opening in the roof of the wigwam allowed smoke to get outside. Families slept on mattresses filled with soft material, such as duck feathers, cattail fuzz, rabbit fur, or balsam branches. Soft blankets were made from bear, rabbit, or deer hide.

Each morning the bedding would be rolled up and placed along the edges of the wigwam for seating.

In the fall the Ojibwe moved near marshes to gather wild rice, known as *manoomin.* They tapped the rice off the stalks into their canoes using long sticks called knockers. Once the rice was harvested, it was dried, roasted, and stored.

When the bitter winter arrived, the Ojibwe were prepared by covering their wigwams with thick furs and animal skins. Campfires burned inside wigwams to help shut out the cold. Men hunted and trapped deer, bear, moose, beaver, and rabbits. Men also fished during the winter through holes cut into ice-covered lakes. The Ojibwe ate the food they stored throughout the seasons.

hide: the skin of an animal

OJIBWE FAMILIES

Children, parents, and sometimes grandparents all shared a wigwam. Several families within the same band often joined each other to make sugar and syrup and to harvest wild rice. During summer months it was common for 300 to 400 Ojibwe to gather together to trade and celebrate. Couples would marry during the gatherings.

Ojibwe women were the cooks. They stored items in containers they made out of bark. They sewed bedding and moccasins out of fur and animal skins.

MANOOMIN

According to an old Ojibwe oral tradition, the Ojibwe were told to find the place where "the food grows on the water." They moved from the east to the shores of the Great Lakes. Manoomin grew in abundance there. The Ojibwe view wild rice as a gift from the Creator and it quickly became fundamental to their diet. Manoomin is also culturally important and is still used in many ceremonies and feasts today.

Traditionally, women and girls wore dresses made out of animal hide. During winter women and girls added leggings and fur coats for warmth. They decorated their clothing with beads and dyed porcupine quills in beautiful patterns. The skills were often passed down and taught to younger girls.

Men wore breechcloths, which are short deerskin clothes worn around the middle of their bodies. In cold weather they added leather leggings, warm shirts, and fur capes or robes. Men typically made bows, arrows, and spears. They made the tools out of animal bones, wood, and stones. Men built canoes out of birch bark. They used the canoes for fishing and wild rice gathering. When boys learned these skills, they felt proud because it meant they were becoming men.

Cradleboards

Ojibwe babies snuggled close to their mothers on cradleboards. A wooden board supported a cloth or deerskin enclosure for the baby. Moss was used to cushion the baby and act as a diaper.

The Ojibwe enjoyed telling stories to each other. Elders and grandparents believed that stories taught children Ojibwe beliefs and values. Young Ojibwe tribe members were taught that honesty, sharing, and treating all living things with respect were important.

elder: older person whose experience makes him or her a leader

Chapter 2

Loss and Change

Life dramatically changed for the Ojibwe in the 1600s when French explorers and fur traders reached Ojibwe territory. The French people wanted beaver and other animal furs in exchange for cloth, cookware, metal tools, knives, and guns. The relationship between the French and the Ojibwe was usually respectful.

Natives were hunting and trapping so many animals, however, that some became scarce. Other Ojibwe resources also started to diminish. Neighboring tribes, the Iroquois and the Dakota, fought the Ojibwe for hunting land.

Many Ojibwe died during the battles. European explorers and Christian missionaries also brought dreadful diseases with them, such as smallpox, which killed many Ojibwe people.

In the mid-1700s England and France battled for control of North American land and trade in the French and Indian War (1754–1763). The Ojibwe sided with France, while the Iroquois were allies of England. A large number of Ojibwe lives were lost, and eventually England won the war. England then controlled more Ojibwe territory and the fur trade.

During the Revolutionary War (1775–1783), the Ojibwe were on the losing side again. American colonists were fighting England for their independence. The Americans won, and many Ojibwe died in the struggle and from diseases. Earlier treaties were ignored, and settlers continued to push westward into Indian country.

American Indians traded beaver pelts for cloth and other goods.

treaty: an official agreement between two or more groups or countries

UNSTEADY RELATIONSHIPS

Starting in the 1820s, the U.S. government signed several treaties with the Ojibwe people and other native tribes. Treaty councils took place in Prairie du Chien and Fond du Lac, Wisconsin. Ojibwe leaders, such as Hole-in-the-Day, helped negotiate the treaties. The Ojibwe thought if they gave up something, they would get something in return.

By the 1850s treaties forced Ojibwe onto reservations, mainly in Michigan, Minnesota, and Wisconsin. The government promised shipments of food and supplies, but the shipments were often late or the food was rotten. In the treaties the tribes had reserved the right to hunt and fish on the land they gave up. But with limited resources the Ojibwe had no choice but to learn to farm the land or they would face starvation. The federal Bureau of Indian Affairs worked to assimilate the Ojibwe and make them more like European Americans.

reservation: an area of land set aside by the government for American Indians; in Canada reservations are called reserves

assimilate: to become familiar with and fit into the culture of another group

In the 1880s children were forced to leave their families and attend schools far away. They were forbidden to speak the Ojibwe language. In some cases children were also given new names. Some Ojibwe were arrested for fishing and hunting in their traditional ways off of the reservations. They were arrested even though their rights had been guaranteed in the treaties. Many missionaries and government officials did not respect Native American customs.

WISCONSIN DEATH MARCH

Starting in the 1840s government officials tried to force all Ojibwe living in Michigan and Wisconsin to relocate to Minnesota. The Ojibwe did not want to move. Several chiefs traveled to Washington, D.C., in 1849 to meet with President Zachary Taylor. They begged the president to allow them to stay on their traditional homelands. But the president refused.

To make the Ojibwe leave Wisconsin and Michigan, government officials sent food and other supplies to Sandy Lake, Minnesota. About 4,000 Ojibwe traveled to Sandy Lake to retrieve their supplies in October 1850. When they arrived, the promised money, food, and other goods were not there.

Government officials hoped the Ojibwe would stay in Sandy Lake permanently. But they wanted to return to their homelands.

By the time they left to go back to Wisconsin and Michigan in early December, it was extremely cold, and snow covered the ground. More than 150 Ojibwe died of disease and starvation in Sandy Lake. Another 250 died on the way home. The tragedy came to be known as the Wisconsin Death March.

Chapter 3

Ojibwe Life Today

Chippewa

The Ojibwe people from six reservations in Minnesota have come together as the Minnesota Chippewa Tribe. There are more than 40,000 tribal members.

WOOD GUNDY

The Anishinaabe people make up the third largest tribe in North America. Today there are about 170,000 Ojibwe in the United States and 60,000 in Canada. Most of the Ojibwe consider themselves woodland people. About half of Ojibwe people live away from reservations, often in cities.

Several reservations and reserves are located on Ojibwe homelands near the Great Lakes.

NATION AND CLAN

There are seven Ojibwe clans. Children belong to their father's clan. The original clans have animal names—crane, loon, fish, bear, deer, martin, and bird. The larger clans are divided into 150 bands in the United States and Canada. Each Ojibwe band has its own government, laws, and services for its members. The leader of a band—the chief—is called a *gimaa*. In the past chiefs were only male, usually a past chief's son or relative. Today Ojibwe chiefs can be men or women.

WINONA LADUKE

Winona LaDuke is well known for advocating for her people and native environmental groups. She is a member of Minnesota's White Earth band of Ojibwe. Non-native people own more than 90 percent of White Earth's original land in northern Minnesota, but LaDuke is seeking change.

After graduating from Harvard University in 1982 with a degree in native economic development, she moved to the White Earth reservation. LaDuke founded the White Earth Land Recovery Project to help reclaim Ojibwe lands that had been promised by an 1867 treaty. The group also works to protect wild rice.

Throughout this struggle LaDuke has been persistent. She has received grants and other money, which have helped recover 1,400 acres (567 hectares) of Ojibwe land. She is executive director of Honor the Earth, which works on native environmental issues. LaDuke ran for vice president in 1996 and 2000 alongside Green Party candidate Ralph Nader.

Tribal governments work hard to help their people. Money generated from casinos on reservation land, for example, benefits each tribe member. The tribal government also uses the *revenue* to help build schools, clinics, and businesses.

CULTURE

The Ojibwe people have adapted to the changes from their past, but they deeply cherish their traditions. They are proud that the Ojibwe language is now taught in schools on and off the reservations. When it is time to gather wild rice or tap maple trees for syrup, Ojibwe living in cities often return home to their reservations. They enjoy continuing these practices with family and friends. Ojibwe people also gather at many powwows. People of all ages sing and dance along to the drumming, celebrating the Anishinaabe culture.

Chippewas of Rama First Nation Annual Powwow in Ontario, Canada

revenue: money that a government gets from taxes and other income sources

Chapter 4

Connecting to the Past

Sharing their traditions with younger generations is important to the Anishinaabe. In Ojibwe culture elders are important sources of learning. They know treasured information about their ancestors, such as stories, crafts, and ceremonies. Elders help pass down this knowledge to young people to help preserve the Ojibwe culture.

Ojibwe children learn their traditional language in reservation schools.

EDUCATION

Many Ojibwe children attend school on a reservation. The reservation schools are respectful of Ojibwe culture and teach students language and history. Children not living on reservations attend public or private schools. Some Ojibwe bands have educational programs to help their members succeed by providing scholarships, extracurricular activities, and library services. Some students stay home to attend college on the reservation. Others leave reservations to go to college. Some universities offer classes in Ojibwe language and culture.

WORK

Today Ojibwe people work on and off reservations. They seek jobs in a variety of fields including manufacturing, construction, entertainment, medicine, and law enforcement. Ojibwe reservations today have many businesses that provide jobs for their tribal members. They include bait shops, campgrounds, gas stations, hotels, and restaurants. On reservations Ojibwe people also support themselves through farming, fishing, forestry, and wild rice gathering. Some reservations rely on tourism and selling goods online, such as wild rice and syrup.

The small hole in the center of the dream catcher is where good dreams come through, according to an Ojibwe legend.

RELIGION

The Ojibwe have long believed that dreams and visions are connections to the spirit world. Children were taught to remember their dreams and to interpret them as messages from the Great Spirit, Gitchi Manitou. Sometimes the Ojibwe people also made webbed dream catchers. They hung them to prevent bad dreams from reaching people.

The Ojibwe people were one of the few tribes to write down their religious beliefs. They drew pictographs on birch bark used as paper. Healers who had special familiarity with sacred plants and Gitchi Manitou kept the birch bark scrolls safe. The respected male and female healers were part of the Midewiwin, the Grand Medicine Society.

MEDICINE DANCE

The Medicine Dance was the most important religious ceremony for the Ojibwe. People gathered in large wigwams with sacred drums and pipes. During the Medicine Dance, newly trained healers offered gifts and feasted on wild rice, fruit, and maple sugar.

In traditional Anishinaabe culture, men or women could be priests in the Midewiwin religion. After one year of training, priests were ready to begin their lives as healers. They could begin healing after the Medicine Dance. Some Ojibwe studied up to 20 years to reach a higher level as a Midewiwin healer.

The Ojibwe still honor their cultural religious traditions. They believe Gitchi Manitou made such elements as fire, wind, water, and rock. From these elements Gitchi Manitou created the sun, Earth, and all other things. The Anishinaabe people also believe everything has a spirit. When gathering food and hunting, Ojibwe offer thanks to the spirit of the land or animal. An offering, such as tobacco or sage, is scattered over a lake or where an animal is killed as a sign of respect to Gitchi Manitou.

Sweat lodges

The Ojibwe cleanse their bodies and spirits during ceremonies inside sweat lodges. Water is poured on hot rocks to produce steam in the small lodges. One at a time, people pray and ask for forgiveness from Gitchi Manitou.

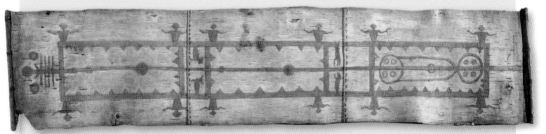

Records of the Midewiwin are inscribed on birch bark scrolls. The oldest known scroll is more than 1,000 years old.

pictograph: picture used as a symbol for a word or phrase
sacred: holy

SPORTS

Ojibwe children play a wide variety of sports and games for fun—and to remember their past. Lacrosse was, and still is, one of the most popular Ojibwe games. Traditionally lacrosse was a rough game, and villages played other villages. Lacrosse was played with two poles. A player could not touch the ball with anything except the netted basket at the end of one of the poles. They could, however, use the pole to hit or trip another player. Players dove after the ball to try to lob it into the goal. Lacrosse has changed through the years, but the game remains an Ojibwe favorite.

School sports

Ojibwe children today play on school sports teams, such as volleyball, basketball, football, and lacrosse.

OLD COMPETITION

The moccasin game is one of the oldest Ojibwe competitions. Traditionally only men were allowed to participate. Players on two teams face each other across a blanket. Drummers play special songs. To play each team needs four tokens or marbles. Three of the marbles are the same color, and one is different. Teams also need four moccasins or pieces of cloth and several sticks. The object of the game is to find the different marble that has been hidden with the other three under the moccasins or cloths. People watching place bets on which team they think will win, while opponents take turns trying to uncover the hidden marble. The winning team has the most points, which are calculated using counting sticks and scoring sticks.

Some food is donated to the Elderly Nutrition Program, which serves and delivers healthy meals to elders on various reservations.

FOOD

What the Ojibwe ate changed with the seasons as bands relocated to be near resources, such as wild rice and maple trees. Maple sugar was used as a seasoning on many types of food. The sugar also played an important role in ceremonies and feasts. Today Ojibwe people continue to hunt and fish. They also still use canoes to gather wild rice. Families plant squash, corn, and potatoes in gardens. Although fruit is not as plentiful as it once was, Ojibwe people still collect wild fruit and berries.

CLOTHING

After contact with Europeans, the Ojibwe people traded some of their soft leather for cotton cloth and wool. But they did not forget their traditions. At special events Ojibwe wear regalia, such as headdresses. For such occasions women braid their hair and weave in colorful ribbons. Men wear brightly colored leggings and deerskin shirts decorated with beads and quills. Women wear long, fringed dresses. Today many Ojibwe people still wear moccasins, the oldest and most traditional symbol of their culture.

traditional Ojibwe regalia at the annual Lac Courte Oreilles Honor the Earth Powwow near Hayward, Wisconsin

regalia: special clothes and decorations for ceremonies and celebrations

CRAFTS

Ojibwe artists are known for their beadwork and quill embroidery. Beads are sewn onto clothing and deerskin bags. Quillwork embroidery with porcupine quills is stitched on birch bark boxes and other items in patterns. The Ojibwe also enjoy making belts out of purple and white beads called wampum. The wampum belts often tell a tribe's story or history. Other traditional Ojibwe crafts include dream catchers, birch bark boxes, and baskets.

Ojibwe beadwork adorns a velvet bag.

MEDICINE

The Anishinaabe relied on medicine men and women for physical and mental healing. Medicine people, called healers, had a number of techniques they used to help prevent or cure illnesses and diseases. Minor illnesses could sometimes be treated with herbal plants or by cleansing in a sweat lodge. Attempts to cure other sicknesses required special ceremonies. Today the Ojibwe still have healers within their bands, but they also visit hospitals and clinics for healthcare.

POWWOWS

Dancing has always been an important part of Ojibwe culture. Long ago family members may have created costumes made from rabbit or deer hides. They would then dance, using movements that looked like a rabbit or a deer. Today this is considered traditional dancing and is often performed at powwows.

There are other types of dancing at powwows too. In a Circle Dance a ring of people dance together using the same movements. A Stomp Dance begins with all dancers kneeling and is a symbol of bravery. The Jingle Dress Dance began as a medicine dance but is now commonly seen at powwows. It is a noisy dance, and the dancers wear bright costumes. The Grass Dance is one of the oldest Ojibwe dances still used at powwows. The dancers sway back and forth, mimicking grass in the wind.

Powwows are an important way to celebrate Ojibwe traditions. A typical powwow gathering can last from several hours to several days with a wide range of events and activities. Dancers compete for prizes. Ojibwe people, both adults and children, ride in parades. A variety of traditional foods are also available at powwows. People sell authentic Ojibwe arts and crafts. The celebrations often attract hundreds of people that come to honor Anishinaabe history.

TIMELINE

Around 900: Ojibwe ancestors begin to migrate west to the Great Lakes.

1615: French explorer Samuel de Champlain encounters the Ojibwe near Lake Huron.

1781–1819: Ojibwe sign various treaties, giving up land in Canada and the northern United States.

1850: Hundreds of Ojibwe die in the Wisconsin Death March.

1854–1867: Various treaties establish Ojibwe reservations in Michigan, Minnesota, and Wisconsin.

1887: The Dawes General Allotment Act passes, which gives about 160 acres (65 hectares) of reservation land to individual tribe members and allows millions of acres of native land to be sold to white settlers.

1889: Treaty at Red Lake allows sale of land surrounding the northern Minnesota reservation and exempts Red Lake from the allotment policy; it is one of the few reservations in the United States not "checker-boarded" with land owned by whites.

1924: The American Indian Citizen Act makes U.S. citizens of all American Indians.

1984: Great Lakes Indian Fish and Wildlife Commission is established to safeguard treaty-guaranteed rights to hunt, fish, and gather wild rice in Michigan, Minnesota, and Wisconsin.

1999: The U.S. Supreme Court upholds the Ojibwe right to hunt, fish, and gather wild rice; the ruling stems from a 1990 lawsuit filed by the Mille Lacs band of Ojibwe against the state of Minnesota.

2009: President Barack Obama signs bill that includes text apologizing to American Indians for "many instances of violence, maltreatment, and neglect."

2015: Ojibwe harvest wild rice off the reservation in northern Minnesota in an on-going treaty dispute with the state.

GLOSSARY

ancestor (AN-sess-tur)—family member who lived a long time ago

assimilate (uh-SIM-uh-layt)—to become familiar with and fit into the culture of another group

band (BAND)—group of related people who live and hunt together

elder (EL-dur)—older person whose experience makes him or her a leader

hide (HYDE)—the skin of an animal

pictograph (PIK-toh-graf)—picture used as a symbol for a word or phrase

regalia (ri-GALE-yuh)—special clothes and decorations for ceremonies and celebrations

reservation (rez-er-VAY-shuhn)—area of land set aside by the government for American Indians; in Canada reservations are called reserves

revenue (REV-uh-noo)—money that a government gets from taxes and other income sources

sacred (SAY-krid)—holy

tradition (truh-DISH-uhn)—custom, idea, or belief passed down through time

treaty (TREE-tee)—an official agreement between two or more groups or countries

READ MORE

Chambers, Catherine. *American Indian Myths and Legends.*
All About Myths. Chicago: Raintree, 2013.

Ramsey, Torren. *Ojibwe.* Spotlight on Native Americans.
New York: PowerKids Press, 2016.

Weil, Ann, and Charlotte Guillain. *American Indian Cultures.*
Global Cultures. Chicago: Heinemann Library, 2013.

INTERNET SITES

FactHound offers a safe, fun way to find Internet sites
related to this book. All of the sites on FactHound have
been researched by our staff.

Here's all you do:

Visit *www.facthound.com*

Type in this code: 9781515702405

 Check out projects, games and lots more at
www.capstonekids.com

CRITICAL THINKING USING THE COMMON CORE

1. Why do you think learning and preserving the Ojibwe language is so important to Anishinaabe people today? (Integration of Knowledge and Ideas)

2. In your opinion, which event or historical time period affected the lives of Ojibwe the most? Why? (Key Ideas and Details)

3. In what ways do Ojibwe people today pay tribute to the cultural customs and traditions of their ancestors? (Key Ideas and Details)

INDEX